ALSO BY THE AMERICAN HEART ASSOCIATION FROM TIMES BOOKS

American Heart Association Low-Fat, Low-Cholesterol Cookbook, Second Edition

American Heart Association Low-Salt Cookbook

American Heart Association Quick & Easy Cookbook

American Heart Association Around the World Cookbook

American Heart Association Kids' Cookbook

American Heart Association Family Guide to Heart Attack: Treatment, Recovery, and Prevention

American Heart Association Family Guide to Stroke: Treatment, Recovery, and Prevention

Living Well, Staying Well: The Ultimate Program to Help Prevent Heart Disease and Cancer (with the American Cancer Society)

American Heart Association Brand Name Fat and Cholesterol Counter, Second Edition

American Heart Association 6 Weeks to Get Out the Fat

American Heart Association Fitting in Fitness

American Heart Association 365 Ways to Get Out the Fat

THE NEW AMERICAN HEART ASSOCIATION COOKBOOK

American Heart Association®

Fighting Heart Disease and Stroke

CLARKSON POTTER/PUBLISHERS
NEW YORK

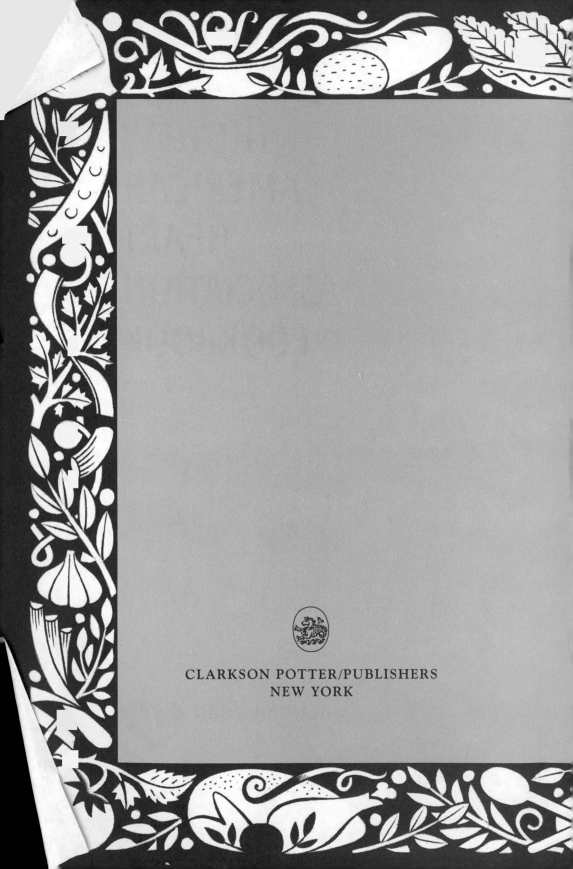